INTERNATIONAL FARMYARD

A LANGUAGE BOOK FOR CHILDREN

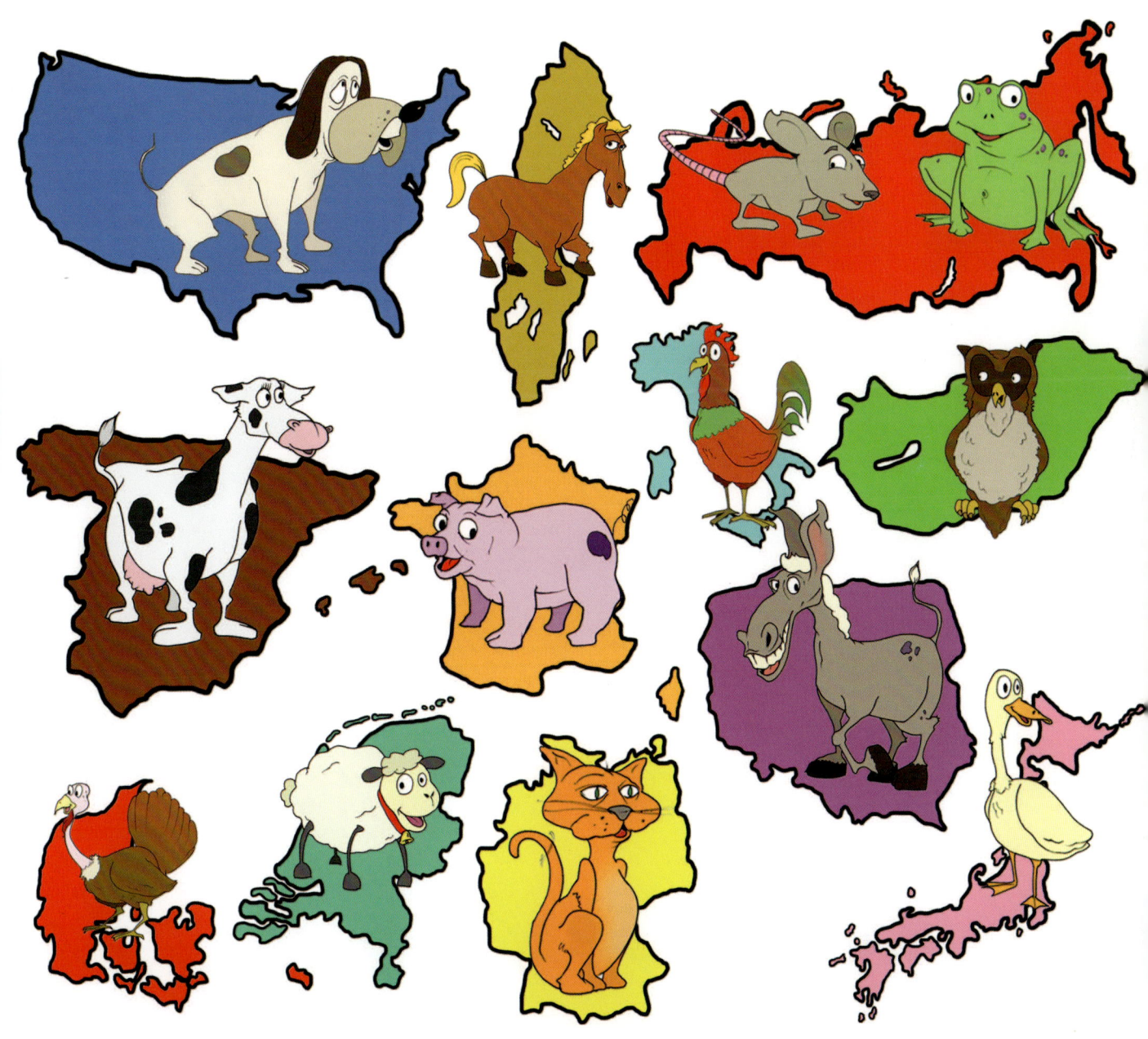

MARY PATRICIA DUBUC

International Farmyard
A Language Book for Children

Copyright © 2013 by Mary Patricia Dubuc

All rights reserved. No part of this book may be reproduced or transmitted in any form or by any means without written permission of the publisher.

Illustrations by Sean Wallace

Cover design by Jacob Kubon

Published by

splatteredinkpress.com

ISBN 978-1-939294-06-7

Acknowledgments

This book was begun with just one page some twenty-five years ago. With many thanks to Tricia L. McDonald and her support, I began working on it again in Feb. 2012. During this time she helpfully guided me to its final completion and publication.

This book is dedicated to all of my Grandchildren Kelley, Katie, Danielle, Jaclyn, Eric, Jessica, Katherine, Emily, and Josh.

UNITED STATES OF AMERICA

"Where are you going?" **WOOF WOOF (wuf wuf)** barked the **DOG** to the **COW**.

"Going to look for **WATER (wa ter)**,"
(moo moo) mooed the **COW** to the **DOG**.

ESPAÑA (Es paan ya)
SPAIN

"Where are you going?" **MUUU (mu uuu)** mooed the **VACA (baa ka)** cow to the **PAVO (pa vo)** turkey.

3

"Going to look for **AGUA (a gua)** water," **CLOU CLOU (clu clu)** gobbled the **PAVO (pa vo)** turkey.

DANMARK (Dan mark)
DENMARK

"Where are you going?" **KLUKKER KLUKKER (kluka kluka)** gobbled the **KALKUN (kal koon)** turkey to the **FÅR (fa)** sheep.

"Going to look for **VAND (vehn)** water," **MAEH MAEH (may may)** bleated the **FÅR (fa)** sheep.

6

NEDERLANDS (Nee der lant)
NETHERLANDS (Dutch Language)

"Where are you going?" **MA (maaa)** bleated the **SCHAPEN (schkapen)** sheep to the **PAARD (paaart)** horse.

"Going to look for **WATER (vata)** water," **HEHEHE (hee-hee-hee)** whinnied the **PAARD (paaart)** horse.

SVERIGE (Sva' dee a)
SWEDEN

"Where are you going?" **IIHAHA (ee ha ha)** neighed the **HÄST (hest)** horse to the **GRIS (ger ese)** pig.

"Going to look for **VATTEN (vaa tun)** water,"
NÖFF NÖFF (nawf nawf) grunted the
GRIS (ger ese) pig.

FRANÇE (Fuans)
FRANCE

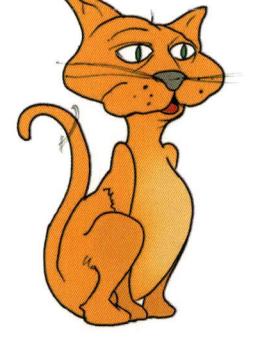

"Where are you going?" **GROIN GROIN (gua gua)** grunted the **PORC (park)** pig to the **SHAT (shat)** cat.

11

"Going to look for the **EAU (oou)** water,"
MIAOU MIAOU (me aw - me aw)
mewed the **SHAT (shat)** cat.

DEUTSCHLAND (Doych laant)
GERMANY

"Where are you going?" **MIOW MIOW** (meow meow) mewed the **KATZE** (katz eh) cat to the **HAHN** (han) rooster.

13

"Going to look for **WASSER (vassa)** water,"
KIKERIKI (key ker e key) crowed the
HAHN (han) rooster.

14

ITALIA (E tal ea)
ITALY

"Where are you going?" **CHICCHIRICHI** (chek-cher-e chee) clucked the **GALLO** (gal lo) rooster to the **MOUSE** (mous eh) mouse.

15

"Going to look for **ACQUA (a cqua)** water," **SQUIT SQUIT (squit squit)** squeaked the **MOUSE (mous eh)** mouse.

ROSSIYA (Ri c ea)
RUSSIA

"Where are you going?" **PI PI PI (peep peep peep)** squeaked the **MYŠ (muush)** mouse to the **LjAGUSKA (le goosh kah)** frog.

17

"Going to look for **VODA (va duh)** water,"
KBA KBA (kva kva) croaked the
LjAGUSKA (le goosh kah) frog.

MAGYARORSZÁG (Myo ro zag)
HUNGARY

"Where are you going?" **BREKEKE (bre ke ke)** croaked the **BÉKA (bay kaw)** frog to the **BAGOLY (baa goy)** owl.

"Going to look for **VÍZ (veez)** water,"
HU HU' HU (hoo hoo' hoo) hooted the
BAGOLY (baa goy) owl.

20

POLAND (Polska)
POLAND

"Where are you going?" **GWIZDALI (hu hu)** hooted the **SOWA (sova)** owl to the **OSIOŁ (ow shau)** donkey.

"Going to look for **WODA (voda)** water,"
EAA EAA (eah eah) brayed the
OSIOŁ (ow shau) donkey.

NIPPON (Ne pon)
JAPAN

"Where are you going?" **HENN (he-nn)** brayed the **NOVA (no va)** donkey to the **AHIRU (a he du)** duck.

23

"Going to look for **MIZU (mee za)** water,"
GAH GAH (cah cah) quacked
the **AHIRU (a he du)** duck.

24

Muuu

HEHEHE

Gah Gah

Woof Woof

Kikeriki

Miaou Miaou

Squit Squit

Hooray!

25

Hu Hu' Hu

Eaa Eaa

Kba Kba

Nŏff Nŏff

Maeh Maeh

Clou Clou

We found the water! 26

Animal Names

ENGLISH	LANGUAGE	TRANSLATION	PRONUNCIATION
COW	SPANISH	VACA	baa ka
TURKEY	SPANISH	PAVO	pa vo
TURKEY	DANISH	KALKUN	kal koon
SHEEP	DANISH	FÅR	fa
SHEEP	DUTCH	SCHAPEN	schkapen
HORSE	DUTCH	PAARD	paaart
HORSE	SWEDEN	HÄST	hest
PIG	SWEDEN	GRIS	ger ese
PIG	FRENCH	PORC	park
CAT	FRENCH	SHAT	shat
CAT	GERMAN	KATZE	katz eh
ROOSTER	GERMAN	HAHN	han
ROOSTER	ITALIAN	GALLO	gal lo
MOUSE	ITALIAN	MOUSE	mous eh
MOUSE	RUSSIAN	MYŠ	muush
FROG	RUSSIAN	LjAGUSKA	le goosh kah
FROG	HUNGARIAN	BÉKA	bay kaw
OWL	HUNGARIAN	BAGOLY	baa goy
OWL	POLISH	SOWA	sova
DONKEY	POLISH	OSIOŁ	ow shau
DONKEY	JAPANESE	NOVA	no va
DUCK	JAPANESE	AHIRU	a he du

Sounds the Animals Make

ENGLISH	LANGUAGE	TRANSLATION	PRONUNCIATION
DOG	ENGLISH	WOOF WOOF	wuf wuf
COW	ENGLISH	MOO MOO	moo moo
COW	SPANISH	MUUU	mu uuu
TURKEY	SPANISH	CLOU CLOU	clu clu
TURKEY	DANISH	KLUKKER KLUKKER	kluka kluka
SHEEP	DANISH	MAEH MAEH	may may
SHEEP	DUTCH	MA	maaa
HORSE	DUTCH	HEHEHE	hee-hee-hee
HORSE	SWEDEN	IIHAHA IIHAHA	ee ha ha
PIG	SWEDEN	NÖFF NÖFF	nawf nawf
PIG	FRENCH	GROIN GROIN	gua gua
CAT	FRENCH	MIAOU	me aw me aw
CAT	GERMAN	MIOW MIOW	meow meow
ROOSTER	GERMAN	KIKERIKI	key ker e key
ROOSTER	ITALIAN	CHICCHIRICHI	chek cher e chee
MOUSE	ITALIAN	SQUIT SQUIT	squit squit
MOUSE	RUSSIAN	PI PI PI	peep-peep-peep
FROG	RUSSIAN	KBA KBA	kva kva
FROG	HUNGARY	BREKEKE	bre ke ke
OWL	HUNGARY	HU HU' HU	hoo hoo' hoo
OWL	POLAND	GWIZDALI	hu hu
DONKEY	POLAND	EAA EAA	eah eah
DONKEY	JAPAN	HENN	he-nn
DUCK	JAPAN	GAH GAH	cah cah

Page Numbers

ENGLISH	LANGUAGE	NUMBER	PRONUNCIATION
1	AMERICAN	ONE	one
2	ENGLISH	TWO	two
3	SPANISH	TRES	tres
4		QUATRO	qua tro
5	DANISH	FEM	fem
6		SEKS	seks
7	DUTCH	ZEVEN	zae fen
8		ACHT	ach t
9	SWEDEN	NIO	ne u
10		TIO	te u
11	FRENCH	ONZE	unz
12		DOUZE	douz
13	GERMAN	DREIZEHN	dri zeen
14		VIERZEHN	feer zeen
15	ITALIAN	QUINDICI	QUEEN dee chee
16		SEDICI	say dee chee
17	RUSSIA	SEMNADSAT	sem nad sits
18		VOSEMNADTSAT	vo sim nad sits

(roll r's in russian)

19	HUNGARY	TIZENKILENC	ti zen kil lantz
20		HÚSZ	hooz
21	POLAND	DWADZIEŚCIA JEDEN	dva descha yeden
22		DWADZIEŚCIA DWA	dva descha dva

(roll r's in polish)

| 23 | JAPANESE | NIZU SAN | nijuu sahn |
| 24 | | NIZU YON | nijuu yohn |

29

Water

WORD	LANGUAGE	TRANSLATION	PRONUNCIATION
WATER	ENGLISH	WATER	wa ter
WATER	SPANISH	AGUA	a gua
WATER	DANISH	VAND	vehn
WATER	DUTCH	WATER	va ta
WATER	SWEDISH	VATTEN	vaa tun
WATER	FRENCH	EAU	oou
WATER	GERMAN	WASSER	vassa
WATER	ITALIAN	ACQUA	a cqua
WATER	RUSSIAN	VODA	vo DUH
WATER	HUNGARY	VÍZ	veez
WATER	POLAND	WODA	voda
WATER	JAPAN	MIZU	mee za

Instructional Guide

Use teaching aides such as flash cards, drawing on the board, overhead projector, Power Point, as well as the book, to illustrate the subject matter being taught.

1. How do you say _____ in _____?

    Ex: water (VATTEN) in Swedish

2. What page number are we reading and what is the language?

    Ex: Four - Quatro (qua tro) in Spanish.

3. What is the name of the animal the turkey is talking to in Danish?

    Ex: (sheep) FÅR.

4. How do you say the water in French?
   Ex: EAU (oou)

5. What color is the pig in English?

6. Children portray sounds of what each animal is saying such as (chek-cher-e-chee) Italian rooster to the Italian mouse (squit –squit).

7. Have children color a picture of the animal(s) teacher is referencing.

8. How do you say the page number (fourteen) in German?

    Ex: Vierzehn (feer zeen).

Sources

www.amazon.com/Animals-Speak-Lila-Prap/dp/0735820589

www.animalport.com

www.eleceng.adelaide.edu.au/personal/dabbott/animal.html

www.en.bab.la/dictionary/english-japanese/

www.forvo.com

www.langtolang.com/ - Langtolang Multilingual Dictionary

www.microsofttranslator.com – Bing Translator

www.omniglot.com

www.paralink.com

www.phrasebase.com

www.poltran.com

www.stars21.com/translator

www.translate.google.com

www.translation.babylon.com

www.wordtranslator.inbox.com/ - Free Word Translation

Polish/Polska Language 30/Phrase Book and 2 Audio Cassettes - A conversation course using a proven self-learning method by Educational Services Teaching Cassettes (1986)

About the Author

International Farmyard is the first published book authored by Mary Patricia Dubuc.

She and her husband Don raised a family of four children.

After working for almost twenty years at the University of Michigan-Dearborn, teaching courses in Stress Reduction Through Yoga, and taking classes, Mary Pat retired.

Both she and her husband Don travelled extensively in the USA and Canada by train during their retirement, visiting both family and friends.

She and her husband moved from Dearborn, Michigan to Spring Lake, Michigan in the year 2003.